COLORING OUR LOVE™

A Therapeutic Affair
By
Shu-Ann Hoo

All inquiries should be addressed to:
OohSA Productions Inc.
shuann2015@gmail.com
ISBN : 978-0-9951516-1-1

Dedicated to my true love, Jeff.

PREFACE

For most of us, Kama Sutra is a mysterious and private encyclopedia for lovemaking meant to unlock the secrets to infinite orgasms while establishing long, meaningful relationships. Different cultures interpret sexual experiences differently, some are conservative to talk about it or that it's dirty to even think about it, while others want to discuss their sexual pleasures with their partners but are sometimes too shy or embarrassed to share with their partners which position would give them their double, triple or infinite 'O's.

Coloring Our Love™ was created with a canonical inventory of carefully hand crafted positions for sexual intercourse and other methods of sensual pleasures, an extension to couple's therapy. The objective of Coloring Our Love™ is to recognize the importance of the quality of our relationship with your partner – to emotionally connect, gain mutual trust and establish a sense of comfort within the relationship which could ultimately lead to the fulfillment of your sexual desires, meant to relax, calm your minds, and set the mood while opening up to each other. Once you create the space to feel, love and explore, you are better able to communicate what you want or crave for, and that gradually takes away the everyday stressors of life as you unwind and destress together, while appreciating each other's company. As you connect with each other, you trigger the release of oxytocin – commonly known as "love hormone" to help you establish a greater sense of intimacy and attachment while colouring together. Releasing oxytocin has potential to treat people with clinical depression, promote feelings of trust, and helps reduce stress. Simply put, it's a love potion that is built just right to make love, not war!

Coloring Our Love™ is a catalyst for couples regardless of where your relationship stands at this point. The ultimate aim of this book is for you to develop a solid, evolving friendship with your partner, for both of you to recognize the comfort you share with each other, making it easy for you to offer more and surrender without reservations in the bedroom and most importantly without being judged. I hope it will take the both of you forever to complete coloring this book...After all, couples who color together, communicate and make love to each other!

With Love,
Shu-Ann

Bend The Rules

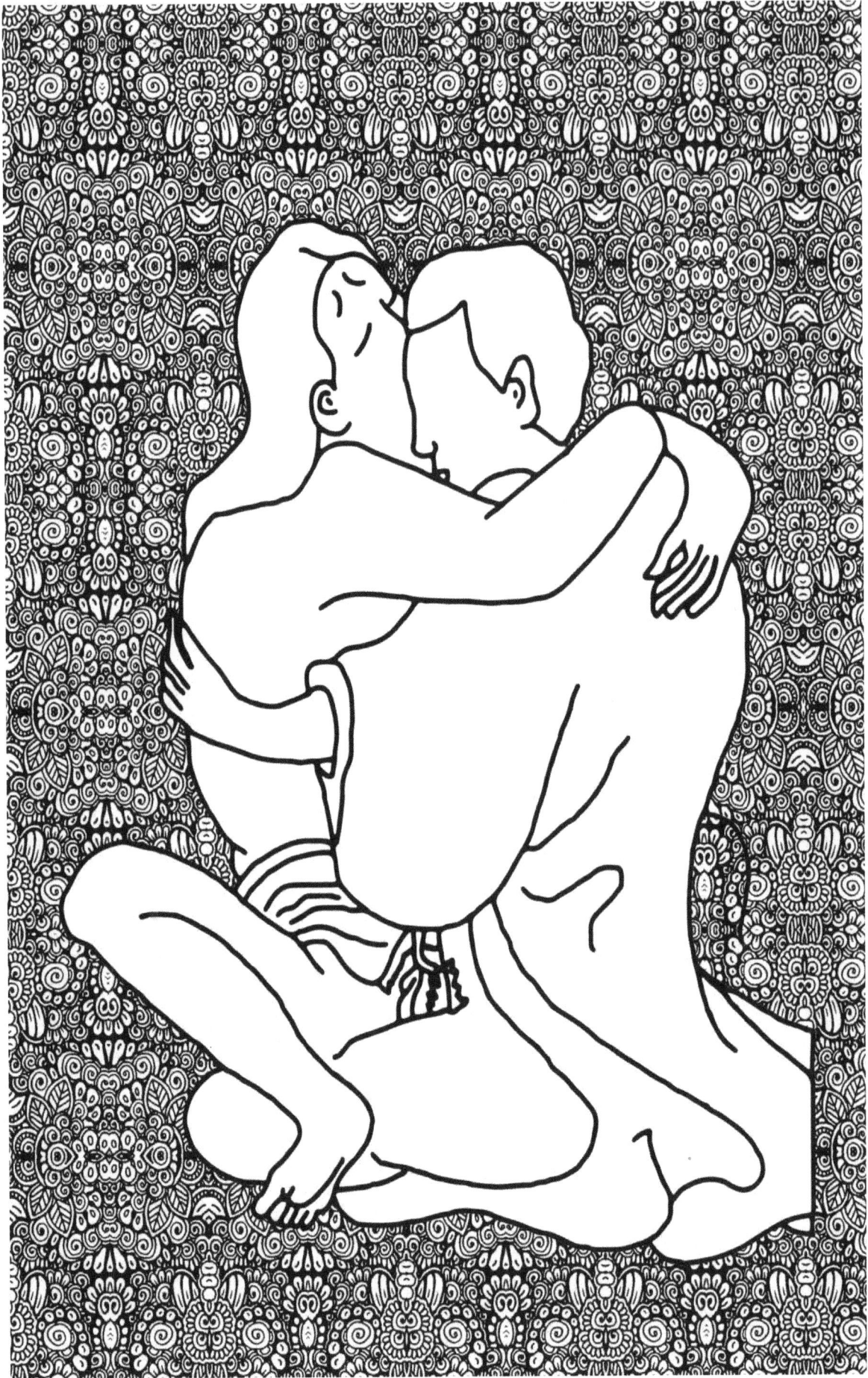

THE HOT SEAT

TOUCH ME WHEN WE'RE DANCING

Love Potion 69

www.ingramcontent.com/pod-product-compliance
Lightning Source LLC
Chambersburg PA
CBHW081553040426

42448CB00016B/3307